ETHAN FROME

In the early years of the 20th century, life on a farm in Massachusetts is not easy. The New England winters are hard; snow and ice cover the fields for months, and the nights are long and cold. For a poor farmer like Ethan Frome, life has few bright moments.

Ethan is a slow, quiet man, but he feels things strongly. He feels the beauty of the world around him – stars shining in a moonless sky, the blue shadows of trees on sunlit snow. He feels the sad loneliness of his life, locked in a loveless marriage to Zeena, a cold, silent woman, whose only interest is her own ill health. Then Zeena's cousin, Mattie Silver, comes to live in the farmhouse, and as the months pass, Ethan feels a new happiness stealing into his life. He loves to watch Mattie's face across the dinner table, to see her sweet smile and hear her soft voice, to walk arm in arm with her across the snowy fields.

His wife Zeena says very little, but her cold, watchful eyes see everything . . .

T0344587

OXFORD BOOKWORMS LIBRARY
Classics

Ethan Frome
Stage 3 (1000 headwords)

Series Editor: Jennifer Bassett
Founder Editor: Tricia Hedge
Activities Editors: Jennifer Bassett and Alison Baxter

EDITH WHARTON

Ethan Frome

Retold by
Susan Kingsley

OXFORD UNIVERSITY PRESS

OXFORD
UNIVERSITY PRESS

Great Clarendon Street, Oxford OX2 6DP

Oxford University Press is a department of the University of Oxford.
It furthers the University's objective of excellence in research, scholarship,
and education by publishing worldwide in

Oxford New York

Auckland Cape Town Dar es Salaam Hong Kong Karachi
Kuala Lumpur Madrid Melbourne Mexico City Nairobi
New Delhi Shanghai Taipei Toronto

With offices in

Argentina Austria Brazil Chile Czech Republic France Greece
Guatemala Hungary Italy Japan Poland Portugal Singapore
South Korea Switzerland Thailand Turkey Ukraine Vietnam

OXFORD and OXFORD ENGLISH are registered trade marks of
Oxford University Press in the UK and in certain other countries

ISBN 978 0 19 479115 1

A complete recording of this Bookworms edition of
Ethan Frome is available

Printed in China

Illustrated by: Paul Fisher Johnson

Word count (main text): 10,700 words

For more information on the Oxford Bookworms Library,
visit www.oup.com/bookworms

CONTENTS

1
Beginnings

❋

If you know Starkfield, Massachusetts, you know the post office there. If you know the post office, you have probably seen Ethan Frome driving up to it in his buggy; and you have probably wondered who he was.

It was there that, several years ago, I saw him for the first time. He was a noticeable figure. His tall, strong body was badly twisted, and much shorter on the right side than on the left. He moved slowly and painfully, pulling himself

His tall, strong body was badly twisted, and he moved slowly and painfully, pulling himself along.

along. Just the few steps from his buggy to the post office were clearly difficult for him. His face had a sad, grim look. It was the face and body of an old man, and I was surprised to hear that he was only fifty-two.

I learnt this from Harmon Gow, a man who knew all the families around Starkfield.

'He's been like that since his bad accident, nearly twenty-four years ago,' said Harmon. 'But Fromes don't die young. Ethan'll live to a hundred, probably.'

'He looks like a dead man already,' I said.

'I guess he's been in Starkfield too many winters,' said Harmon. 'Most smart people get out of here.'

'Why didn't he get out?' I asked.

'He had to stay and take care of his family – first his father got hurt, then his mother fell sick, then his wife.'

'And then the accident?'

Harmon gave a little smile. 'That's right. He had to stay then.'

Ethan Frome used to drive in from his farm every day at about midday, and because I picked up my mail at about the same time, I often saw him. He came to the post office only for a newspaper, and sometimes for a packet from a medicine company for 'Mrs Zeena Frome'. Starkfield people understood that he did not want to stop and talk, and on most days Frome climbed slowly back into his buggy and drove away without a word to anyone.

At that time my company had sent me on an engineering job near Starkfield, and I was staying at the home of a lady called Mrs Ruth Hale. Before she was married, her name had been Ruth Varnum, but her husband Ned Hale was now dead, and she had returned to live with her mother in the Varnum home. It was a grand house, large and white, with tall dark trees outside. Although it was clear that the Varnums no longer had much money, theirs was still the finest house in the village.

Ruth Hale enjoyed talking about her neighbours, and I hoped that she could tell me more about Ethan Frome. But when I asked her, she just looked unhappy and said in a low voice:

'Yes, I knew them both . . . it was awful . . .'

I asked other people, and everybody in Starkfield agreed that Ethan Frome had had more troubles in his life than most people. But nobody explained why he had that sad, grim look on his face.

In the end, I learnt the story, piece by piece, from several people. As often happens, the story was different each time, but I slowly began to put it together. And my interest in Ethan Frome grew stronger when – a little later – I met the man himself.

It happened like this. Every day I had to travel about three miles to the station, where I got my train to work. I usually hired a horse from Denis Eady, the rich village shopkeeper. But in the middle of winter his and most of the other Starkfield horses caught an illness. For a day or two I could not find a horse to hire anywhere, until Harmon Gow had an idea.

'Why don't you ask Ethan Frome to drive you?' he said. 'His horse ain't sick, and he needs a dollar or two. That Frome farm and saw-mill don't make enough money to keep a cat alive.'

So Ethan Frome agreed to drive me, and every day for a week I sat beside him in his sleigh as his thin horse pulled us over the hard snow to the station. Then, in the icy evenings, he brought me back to Starkfield.

He was not unfriendly, but during the hour's drive he never turned to look at me, and spoke very little. Once I said something about Florida and he told me that he had been there. Another time he showed interest in a science book of mine, which I had left in his sleigh by mistake in the morning. But most of the time Frome drove without a word, and I began to feel that he was like the land around him. This sad, silent man and the snow-covered fields had the same kind of cold loneliness. Anything warm and alive inside him was locked away, under the deep icy cold of too many Starkfield winters.

After about a week, we were driving back one night in terrible weather. Heavy snow was falling, hiding everything in a soft white cloud, and the air had an icy coldness. The old horse was getting tired, and I got out to walk beside him, but I found it hard to keep moving.

After a time Frome looked into the darkness and said:

'That's my place down there. We've had enough of this.'

I understood that he was offering me a bed for the night, and we turned down towards the poor, lonely-looking

Heavy snow was falling, and the air had an icy coldness.

farmhouse. After I had helped him put away the sleigh and take care of the horse, we fought our way through the snow to the front of the house. I followed him inside, and from behind a door on our right I heard a woman's voice, a thin, high, whining voice.

Frome opened the door of the room. 'Come in,' he said to me, and as he spoke, the whining voice fell silent.

That was the night when I began to understand Ethan Frome, and to put together his story . . .

2
Coming home from the dance

It was a cold, clear night, and the village lay under deep snow. Bright, icy stars shone from a dark sky down on the silent whiteness below.

Young Ethan Frome walked quickly down the empty, moonlit street. He passed Eady's fine new shop and the Varnums' house with its two tall black trees. Below that was the slope of the Corbury road. On clear nights this was often full of young people coasting down, laughing and shouting as they went. But there was not a sound from the icy slope as Ethan passed by. Tonight all Starkfield's life was in a room in the church. Its windows sent yellow light across the snow, and the sound of dance music flowed out into the still midnight air. Ethan hid in the shadows outside the church, and looked in through the nearest window.

The room was hot, bright, and filled with young men and girls. The music had finished, and people were getting ready to leave. Suddenly, a lively young man with thick black hair jumped into the middle of the floor. He went into the crowd and pulled out a young girl. She was dark-haired, and had a bright red scarf around her head. The music started again, and soon the floor was alive with dancing figures.

Outside in the cold, Ethan's heart was beating fast. His eyes followed the girl's red scarf and cloud of brown hair as she danced in faster and faster circles. The young man was Denis Eady, the son of Starkfield's most successful shopkeeper. Denis's own success with the young women of the village was well known. Ethan watched jealously as Mattie, the dark-haired girl, held Eady's hands and smiled at him with her dark, shining eyes.

'How can she look at him like that?' Ethan wondered unhappily. 'Doesn't she realize what he is like?'

Ethan used to walk into Starkfield to fetch home his

Ethan watched jealously.

wife's cousin, Mattie Silver, on the few evenings when some
chance of amusement brought her to the village. Mattie had
been with the Fromes for a year now. She lived with them
in their lonely farmhouse and helped Ethan's wife, Zeena,
with the housework. Ethan had liked the warm, smiling girl
from the moment that she arrived. She brought hope and
life and brightness into his home, like someone lighting a
fire in a cold room. But she had more than brightness; Ethan
found that she loved the beauty of the natural world around
them. Here at his side, living under his roof and eating his
bread, was someone who felt the same wonder as he did.
He could tell her things and show her things – the bright
stars in the clear night sky, birds flying over golden fields,
the blue shadows of trees on sunlit snow. And he knew that
these things gave Mattie and him the same feelings of deep,
silent happiness.

But now those feelings seemed so far away. He watched
Mattie's laughing face as she flew round and round the
room, and he felt lonely and unhappy. Then he remembered
a fear that he had tried to forget. His wife was a cold, silent
woman who noticed everything but said very little. Her
only real interest was her own ill health. But recently she
had started to complain more and more about Mattie's
housework, and to say things which worried Ethan.

'I'll need someone to help me when Mattie leaves,' she
had said suddenly one morning.

'Oh, Mattie'll never leave us while you need her,' he replied.

His wife lay in bed and watched as he got dressed. 'If a

poor girl like her has a chance to marry a smart boy like Denis Eady, I ain't going to stop her,' she said in her flat, whining voice. 'The doctor says I can't manage on my own, so we'll need to hire a girl.'

Life without Mattie! Ethan could not think of it. Her voice, her sweet smile, her gentle arm in his arm during those night walks back to the farm – these were the only things which mattered in his world. Had he been stupid to think that Zeena would not notice his interest in Mattie? He had not thought about it before, but now, as he stood in the darkness outside the church, he remembered other things that Zeena had said, and his fear grew . . .

The dancers, now in their thick coats and scarves, came out into the cold night air. Ethan heard Mattie's voice in the crowd, and he stepped back into the shadows, suddenly afraid to speak to her. The crowd quickly disappeared, and Mattie stood alone outside the church, looking around her. Then a man's figure appeared.

'Nobody to walk you home, Matt? What a pity! But ain't I lucky that I got my dad's horse and sleigh down here waiting for us? Come on, let's take a ride!'

The girl said nothing, but stood still, watching, while Denis Eady went to untie the horse. In the shadows, Ethan too watched and waited, with his heart beating fast. Mattie held his life in her hands. Eady got into the sleigh and called to Mattie to join him. Then she turned and ran up the slope.

'Goodbye! Have a lovely ride!' she called back.

Eady laughed and followed her up the slope in his sleigh.

After a moment he jumped down and tried to put his arm through hers. She stepped quickly out of the way, and Ethan's sudden fear turned to happiness. A moment later he heard the sound of Eady's sleigh going away, and saw Mattie walking alone across the snow.

He caught up with her by the Varnums' trees. She turned round, surprised.

'Oh!' she said. 'I thought maybe you couldn't come.'

'If you thought I couldn't come, why didn't you ride back with Denis Eady?' he answered.

'Oh, how did you know?' she cried. 'Where were you? I never saw you!'

They stood in the dark shadows of the trees, and their laughing voices ran together like water dancing down from the mountains in springtime. He put his arm through hers, but neither of them moved. Ethan wished he could stand there with her all night in the blackness. Mattie took a few steps forward and then stopped, looking down the icy slope of the Corbury road.

'There were lots of people coasting this evening,' she said. 'Ned Hale and Ruth Varnum almost crashed into the big tree down there. It's so dangerous, that tree.'

'You'd be safe with me, Matt,' replied Ethan. 'Would you like to come coasting some night? We could come tomorrow if there's a moon.'

'Oh, yes. How lovely!'

They walked along in silence, but then all Ethan's jealous fears returned.

'*There were lots of people coasting this evening.*'

'I guess it's natural that you're going to leave us,' he said at last.

'Leave? You mean Zeena ain't happy with me? I know I ain't so strong or so smart, but I want to try, I really do.'

'So you don't want to leave us, Matt?'

'Where could I go?' she whispered, almost crying.

Her answer made Ethan sad and happy at the same time. They continued their walk, with the dark, starry sky above them, and the quiet, lonely fields all around. At the entrance to Ethan's farmland they passed by the Frome graves. Ethan had always felt that the gravestones were looking at him and saying 'We never got out of Starkfield. Why should you?' But now he didn't want to escape. All he wanted was to be with Mattie, and some day to lie under that cold ground with Mattie beside him. Ethan was happy now, in his world of dreams. For the first time he put his arm around Mattie. She let it stay there, and they walked up to the farmhouse.

The house was dark and quiet. Zeena always went to bed early. On the nights when they came back late, she used to lock up the house and hide the key outside the kitchen door. Ethan felt for the key under the usual stone.

'Matt, the key's not there!' he said. This had never happened before. They began to look for it in the darkness. Suddenly there was a sound inside the house. They heard a step on the stairs and saw light under the door. Then the door opened, and Ethan saw his wife.

She stood in the dark doorway, a tall thin woman with a blanket round her shoulders. She held a lamp in one hand,

and its light threw strange shadows onto her thin lined face. She said nothing, and they stepped into the kitchen. It was deadly cold, like a grave. Ethan shook the snow off his boots.

'I guess you forgot us,' he said, looking at Zeena.

'No. I just felt too bad. I couldn't sleep.'

'I'm sorry,' said Mattie. 'Can I do anything to help, Zeena?'

'No, there's nothing you can do.' Zeena turned away from

'I guess you forgot us,' Ethan said.

her. 'And why couldn't you shake that snow off outside?' she said to her husband.

They left the kitchen, and the two women went towards the stairs. 'If I go up now, Mattie'll see me go into the bedroom with Zeena,' thought Ethan. 'And I don't want that, not tonight.'

'I think I'll stay down here a bit longer. I've got some paperwork to do,' he said.

'What, now?' said Zeena. 'You'll die of cold.'

Ethan did not answer, but turned back towards the kitchen. Then he saw the look in Mattie's eyes. Was it a look of warning?

'I guess you're right. It is awful cold down here,' he agreed. With his head down, he slowly followed his wife up to their bedroom.

3
A visit to the doctor

❋

The next morning was cold and bright. Ethan was down at his saw-mill early because he had to take some wood to the village builder that day. The winter sun burned red in a clear sky, and the sunlight danced over the bright, snowy fields, leaving deep blue shadows under the trees.

Ethan's thoughts were always clearest when he was working in the quiet morning air. Last night, after the bedroom door had closed behind them, Zeena had taken her medicine and gone to bed without a word. Ethan lay next to her, watching the light from under Mattie's door, and thinking. Why had he not kissed her on the walk home? He remembered her soft lips in the moonlight. Now, in the clear morning sunshine, he could still see her face. He could see it in the red sky and in the bright shining snow.

Mattie was the daughter of Orin Silver, a cousin of Zeena Frome's. Silver's medicine company had seemed successful, and he had lived like a rich man. But when he died, his wife and daughter had a terrible surprise. They discovered that he had borrowed thousands of dollars which he could not pay back. This awful news killed Mrs Silver immediately. He had also lost money which belonged to his brothers and sisters, so there was nobody in the family who wanted to help poor Mattie. The twenty-year-old girl was alone in the world, without money and without friends. She was not strong, and she had never studied or learnt to do a job. So Mattie came to Starkfield to work, without pay, in her cousin Zeena's home. At first Zeena often complained about the girl's work. Then, as the months went by, Mattie grew stronger and found the work easier. Zeena had more time to think about her illnesses, and life under the Fromes' roof became more peaceful.

But now, Zeena's strange silent looks, the warning in Mattie's eyes last night . . . Ethan was sure that something was wrong. By midday the wood was all loaded, ready to take to Andrew Hale the builder. But Ethan decided to go

Why had he not kissed her on the walk home?

home. If there was going to be trouble, he wanted to be there. So Ethan and Jotham Powell, his hired man, walked through the fields back to the house.

When they entered the kitchen, Mattie was making coffee. Zeena was sitting at the table, wearing her best brown dress and a tall hat. A suitcase stood beside her.

'Where're you going, Zeena?' asked Ethan, surprised.

'My pains are getting really bad. I'm going over to my aunt's in Bettsbridge for the night, and tomorrow I'll see that new doctor,' she answered. 'If you're too busy, I suppose you can let Jotham Powell drive me to the station.'

Ethan said nothing. He was lost in his own thoughts. He realized that, for the first time, he and Mattie would be alone for the night. He looked at Mattie. Was she thinking the same thing? Then he looked at his wife's thin, lined, bloodless face. Zeena was thirty-five, only seven years older than he was, but she was already an old woman.

'Of course Jotham'll take you,' he said at last. 'I can't do it myself, because I've got to get the money for the wood from Andrew Hale.'

This was a lie. Andrew Hale never paid immediately, but Ethan really had no wish to make the long, slow journey to the station with his miserable wife at his side.

Zeena made no reply, and soon afterwards she left with Jotham. Ethan picked up his coat and stood for a moment in the doorway. 'See you later, Matt,' he said.

It was warm and bright in the kitchen. The sun shone in on the flowering pot plants by the window, and the cat sleeping in a chair. Mattie looked up from her housework. 'See you later, Ethan,' she said happily.

All the way down to the village Ethan thought of his return to Mattie that night. Without Zeena, his house seemed more like a home. And as he drove through the snowy fields, this usually silent man began to sing.

Ethan Frome had not always been so quiet and lonely. As a student he had liked being among happy, friendly, young people. He had enjoyed his science studies and wanted to become an engineer. But after his father's accident and death, Ethan had to leave his studies and return home. Life was hard for him, working alone on the poor farm and unsuccessful saw-mill. Then his mother fell ill, and became more and more silent. Sometimes she used to say a few crazy words, but for most of the time she refused to speak at all. So with each long, cold Starkfield winter, the silence and loneliness round Ethan grew deeper.

As his mother came towards her last illness, Ethan's cousin Zeena arrived to take care of her. It was wonderful to hear another person's voice in the house again, and Zeena was an excellent nurse and housekeeper. Old Mrs Frome finally died one dark winter's day, and the idea of being alone again filled Ethan with fear. He was grateful to Zeena for all that she had done, and he asked her to stay and marry him. They had at first planned to sell the farm and move to the town. But it was hard to find a buyer, and Ethan soon realized that his wife could not live in a place where she was not someone 'important'. In less than a year her 'sickliness' appeared; then she too fell silent. Her strange, wordless looks worried Ethan. Was she going a little crazy, like his mother? What thoughts and plans were hidden behind her cold eyes?

But that afternoon, as Ethan drove to the village with his sleigh full of wood for the builder, he felt less afraid. Zeena had gone away to Bettsbridge, with all her thoughts on her own health. And tonight he had an evening alone with Mattie. But there was still one worry – the lie about the money from Andrew Hale. He knew that Zeena would want to know where it was.

When Ethan arrived at the builder's, Hale invited him into his office to sit down and get warm. He was a large, red-faced and likeable man, an old friend of Ethan's family. Ethan did not know how to begin, but at last he managed to ask Hale for the first fifty dollars towards this winter's wood. The builder was surprised. He always paid at the end of three months, never before. He refused in his warm, friendly way, and then asked:

'Look, you ain't got money problems, have you?'

'No, not at all,' replied Ethan, very embarrassed.

The afternoon had turned into a cold grey evening by the time Ethan left the builder's. He heard the sound of sleigh-bells, and Denis Eady drove past, shouting 'Hello, Ethe!' Eady was going towards the Frome farm. Did he know that Zeena had gone? Was he going there to spend some time alone with Mattie? Ethan felt wildly jealous, then moments later was ashamed of his feelings.

By the Varnum house Ethan saw two figures standing together under the trees. He heard a kiss, and a surprised 'Oh!' as he passed by. Two happy lovers, kissing where he had stood with Mattie the night before. But unlike him, Ruth Varnum and Ned Hale didn't need to hide their feelings. How lucky they were!

As night fell, Ethan passed by the Frome gravestones and drove up to the farmhouse. A light shone in a room upstairs.

'She's getting herself ready for supper,' he thought.

4
An evening together
❋

Ethan went up to the kitchen door, and found that it was locked. He called 'Hello, Matt!' but there was no answer. He stood in the darkness and waited. After a moment he heard a sound on the stairs, and saw light round the door. And just like the night before, the door opened and there stood a woman with a lamp in her hand. The lamplight shone on the milky whiteness of Mattie's young skin, on her soft lips and shining dark eyes. She smiled gently, and stepped to the side to let Ethan come in.

The kitchen was warm and welcoming. On the table were cakes and fruit in a bright red glass dish, and the cat was lying lazily in front of a warm fire.

'Well, Matt, any visitors?' asked Ethan.

'Just one,' replied Mattie, laughing. A black cloud came down over Ethan's world.

'Who was that?'

She looked at him and laughed again. 'Jotham Powell. He came in and asked for a drop of coffee.'

The blackness lifted and Ethan's world grew bright again.

The kitchen was warm and welcoming.

'Well, I hope you gave him some,' he said, then added, 'I suppose Zeena got to the station in time?'

Zeena's name brought an immediate coolness into the kitchen. After a few moments Mattie said: 'I guess it's about time for supper,' and they sat down.

But they still felt uncomfortable – Zeena seemed to be in the room with them, with her cold eyes and strange looks. They ate in embarrassed silence, then began to talk about the weather.

As they were speaking, the cat climbed quietly onto the table and started to move towards the milk-jug. When they saw it, they both reached forwards at once, their hands meeting on the jug. Ethan kept his hand on Mattie's a few seconds longer than was necessary. At that moment the cat suddenly jumped backwards and knocked into the red glass dish. The dish fell to the floor with a crash.

'Oh, Ethan,' Mattie cried. 'It's all in pieces! What will Zeena say? It was her very best dish!'

'Don't worry. I'll get another one.'

'You'll never find one! It was a wedding present from her aunt in Philadelphia. That's why she never uses it. I had to climb up to get it from the top of her cupboard! Oh, Ethan, what shall I do?'

She began to cry, and her tears seemed to burn into Ethan's heart.

'Oh, Matt, don't cry! Please don't cry!' he said softly.

They looked at the bits of red glass lying like the broken pieces of their evening. Ethan picked them up and walked

'Oh, Ethan, what will Zeena say? It was her very best dish!'

out of the kitchen to the hall. Reaching up his long arm, he put the broken pieces at the top of the cupboard and arranged them carefully. From below nobody could see that the dish was broken.

'I'll get some glue to mend it tomorrow,' thought Ethan. 'Zeena won't look at it for months, and I'm sure I'll find another one somewhere.'

He went back to the kitchen. 'It's all right, Matt,' he said. 'Let's finish supper.'

After the meal Mattie cleared the table and Ethan went out to see the cows. The world was dark and still outside. When he came back, Mattie had pushed his chair near the fire and had seated herself by the lamp with a bit of sewing. He sat down, feeling warm and dreamy and at peace with the world. The only trouble was that he could not see Mattie from where he sat. But he felt too lazy to move and after a moment he said: 'Come over here and sit by the fire.'

Mattie got up and sat opposite him in Zeena's rocking-chair. He looked at the chair and for a moment he saw his wife's grim face there. Mattie seemed to feel uncomfortable too. After a while she got up, saying, 'I can't see to sew,' and went back to sit by the lamp.

The cat jumped into the empty rocking-chair, and Ethan moved his own chair a little. Now he could see Mattie as she sat and sewed in the soft lamplight. A deep quiet came over the kitchen. The 'tick-tick' of the clock was the only sound in the room, and the smoke from Ethan's pipe and the smell of Mattie's flowering plants filled the air.

They began to talk easily of everyday things. It all seemed so comfortable and so peaceful. Ethan began to dream that they always spent their evenings like this . . .

'This was the night when we were going coasting,' he said after a while.

She smiled back at him. 'I guess you forgot!'

'No, I didn't forget. It's too dark tonight, but we can go tomorrow if there's a moon.'

'That would be lovely, Ethan!' Mattie laughed happily, and her eyes shone in the lamplight. Ethan loved the way that her face changed as she talked, like a field of grass moving under a gentle summer wind.

'It's too dangerous on a dark night like this,' he went on. 'You've got to keep your eyes open on that slope, you know, Matt. That's a dangerous corner down by that big tree. You could crash right into it if you're not careful.' Then he added: 'I guess we're fine here, aren't we?'

'Yes, we're fine here,' agreed Mattie in a soft, sweet voice. Ethan put down his pipe and pulled his chair up to the table. He touched the end of her piece of sewing.

'Say, Matt, guess what I saw tonight? Your friends kissing under the Varnum trees.'

Mattie's face turned bright red. 'That'll be Ruth and Ned,' she answered, looking down at her sewing. Ethan felt embarrassed too. Last night on their walk home he had put his arm around Mattie, and had wanted to kiss her. But tonight, in the warm lamplit room, she seemed so much further away.

'I guess they'll get married soon,' said Ethan. 'And then maybe you'll be next.'

'Why do you say that?' she replied in a low voice. 'Is it because Zeena doesn't want me to stay?'

'What do you mean?' asked Ethan, afraid again.

'I thought that last night she seemed . . . Oh, I don't know. Nobody knows what Zeena thinks. She hasn't said anything to you, has she?'

He shook his head. 'No, not a word.'

'I guess it was nothing then. Let's not think about it,' said Mattie, and went on with her sewing.

Ethan watched her in silence. Then he gently took hold of

the other end of her piece of sewing. Mattie's warmth seemed to flow along it towards him. Could she feel the answering warmth from his own hand? They sat like this for a few moments, then Ethan heard a sound behind him. The cat had jumped down from Zeena's chair, and because of the sudden movement the empty chair had started a ghostly rocking.

'I've been in a dream,' thought Ethan.

'Zeena'll be in that chair herself this time tomorrow,' thought Ethan. 'I've been in a dream, and this is the only evening we'll ever have together . . .' The return to the real world filled him with pain, and he suddenly felt very tired.

Mattie looked at him, and for a moment he saw fear cross her face. He held onto her sewing and kissed the end of it softly. She pulled it slowly from his lips and put it away. It was eleven o'clock.

'Is the fire all right?' she asked in a low voice.

They checked the fire, moved the plant pots away from the cold window, and put out the lamp.

'Goodnight, Matt,' he said, as she put her foot on the first step of the stairs.

'Goodnight, Ethan,' she answered, and went up.

When the door of her room had closed, he remembered that he had not even touched her hand.

5
Zeena's news
❋

The next morning Jotham Powell came round early to help load some more wood. Ethan could still feel inside him the sweetness of the evening before, and he tried hard not to show his happiness.

He did not know why he felt so happy. There was no reason for it, because nothing had changed in his life or in Mattie's.

But their evening together had given him a dream – a picture of life with Mattie at his side.

He wanted to load the wood quickly and then drive it down to Starkfield, where he could buy the glue to mend the broken dish. He was sending Jotham to fetch Zeena from the station after dinner, so they needed to work fast. But the morning went badly. A wet snow had fallen in the night, and the roads were like glass. One of his horses fell and cut its leg. Icy rain started to fall, making the loading slow and difficult. It was after midday when they finished.

Immediately after dinner, Ethan put his coat on again. Jotham was drying his wet feet by the fire and Mattie was washing the dishes.

'I'll be back early,' Ethan said to Mattie in a low voice. He was afraid to say more in front of Jotham, but he thought that Mattie understood him.

The journey down to the village was long and slow, with his two old horses pulling their heavy load over the snow and ice underfoot. By the time he had unloaded the wood and managed to buy the glue, it was already late afternoon. On the way back the rain began again, turning to ice as it fell on the snow and making the road even more glassy and dangerous. Once or twice Ethan heard sleigh-bells and turned round, afraid that Jotham and Zeena were coming up behind him. But for most of the journey he just looked grimly into the falling rain, as his tired horses made their way up the hill.

At last he arrived home and hurried into the kitchen. Mattie was alone.

Icy rain started to fall, making the loading slow and difficult.

'Look, Matt,' he cried, 'I've got the glue to mend the dish with! Quick, let me get it!'

'Oh, Ethan – Zeena's back!' she said in a whisper, holding onto his arm.

Ethan looked round the kitchen, which looked cold and unwelcoming in the wintry evening light.

'How is she?' he asked, in the same low whisper.

'I don't know. She didn't say anything, she just went straight upstairs.'

Ethan put the glue back in his pocket. 'Don't worry. I'll come down and mend the dish in the night,' he said.

Then, just as she had done the evening before, Mattie said: 'I guess it's about time for supper.'

Ethan called Zeena, but there was no answer. He went up to the bedroom, and pushed open the door. In the darkness he saw Zeena's figure sitting by the window, still wearing her travelling dress.

'Well, Zeena, supper's ready. Ain't you coming?'

'I don't think I could eat a thing,' she replied, then turned her head towards him. 'I'm much sicker than you think.'

'I hope that's not so, Zeena.'

'The doctor says I mustn't do anything at all in the house. So we'll have to get a hired girl.'

'A hired girl?'

'Yes. My aunt's found me one already. She's coming tomorrow afternoon.'

'Why didn't you tell me what you planned to do?' he asked angrily. 'Where do you think I'll get the money to pay her?'

'How did I know what the doctor would say? I'm ashamed to have a husband like you, Ethan Frome. I lost my health taking care of your own mother! Marrying me was the least that you could do after—'

'Zeena!'

The darkness between them was filled with anger. It was their first moment of open fighting in their sad seven years together. Ethan felt ashamed, and tried to speak more calmly.

'You know I don't have the money, Zeena. She'll have to go back.'

'What about that fifty dollars from Andrew Hale?'

He remembered the lie he had told the day before.

'I guess that was a mistake.'

'You mean you ain't going to get it?'

'No. I'm sorry, Zeena. You're a poor man's wife. But I'll do the best I can to help you.'

'Oh, I guess we'll manage,' she said more gently. 'And without Mattie's food to pay for—'

'Without Mattie's—?' he began.

Zeena laughed. It was a strange sound. He couldn't remember hearing her laugh before.

'You didn't think Mattie was staying, did you?'

'But you can't send her away – she's your cousin.'

'Well, we can't keep two girls here.'

Ethan could not believe what he was hearing.

'Ethan – Zeena! Supper's ready!' Mattie called brightly from downstairs.

Ethan felt angry and helpless. 'But where will she go? A

poor girl with no friends or money . . .

'She's been here long enough. We've kept her for over a year now, and it's time for her to go.'

Ethan looked at his wife with eyes full of hate. It was an angry, bitter hate. It was a hate which had grown during years of hard work, hopeless poverty, and broken dreams. This woman had destroyed all his hopes. She had taken everything

Ethan looked at his wife with eyes full of hate.

from him, and now wanted to take the one beautiful thing left in his life. He made a sudden, violent movement towards her, then stopped.

'I don't think I'll come down,' said Zeena calmly. 'I guess I'll just lie on the bed a while.'

Ethan went downstairs to the kitchen, and Mattie gave him a plate of food. He took a mouthful, then pushed the plate away.

'What's the matter, Ethan? Doesn't it taste right?'

'It's fine, Matt. Only I—' He stood up quickly.

She looked at him with frightened eyes. 'I *knew* there was something wrong. What is it, Ethan? What is it?'

He took her in his arms and found her lips at last. He kissed and kissed her. He was lost in the sweetness of her lips. Then she pulled away from him, her face white with fear, and he cried out:

'You can't go, Matt! I'll never let you go!'

'Go . . . go?' she whispered. 'Must I go? Ethan, what has happened? Is Zeena angry with me?'

He told her what the doctor had said. Mattie looked so small and helpless. His heart ached for her, and he wanted to hold her in his arms again. They were silent for a long while, then Mattie said in a low voice:

'Don't be too sorry, Ethan.'

'Oh, Matt – Matt – where'll you go?'

'Maybe I'll get something to do in town.' But they both knew that she had little chance of finding a job. There were too many people looking for work in the towns, and there were no jobs that Mattie could do. And Ethan knew what happened to girls who had no job, no money, and no friends . . . He sat down in despair, and hid his face in his hands.

Then they heard Zeena's footsteps on the stairs. She came down wearing her usual dress. Then she sat down in her usual seat, and took a large plateful of food. She ate well, and talked in an everyday way about the illnesses of her friends and family in Bettsbridge. As she spoke, she looked at Mattie with a small smile on her thin lips. When supper was finished, she stood up and said:

'That meal's given me a stomach-ache. I think I'll go and look for the stomach medicine that I bought last year.'

She left the room. Ethan's and Mattie's eyes met, full of silent despair. The kitchen looked as warm and peaceful as the night before, but now everything had changed. Then suddenly Zeena was back, her face burning with anger. In her hands she held the broken pieces of the red glass dish.

'I want to know who did this,' she said in a shaking voice.

'I can tell you. It was the cat,' answered Ethan after a few moments.

'The *cat*? How did the cat get into my hall cupboard?'

'Oh, Zeena, it was my fault, not Ethan's!' cried Mattie. 'I got it down from your cupboard. I – I wanted the supper table to look pretty.'

'You wanted the supper table to look pretty! So you took my very best dish, the one that I never, ever use. Not for visitors, not for anyone. You're a bad girl, Mattie Silver,

34

In her hands Zeena held the broken pieces of the red glass dish.

just like your father. I always knew you were bad – that's why I hid my things from you. And now you've taken the thing that I cared for the most—' Tears ran down her thin, yellowish face. Then she left the room, carrying the pieces of broken glass like a dead body.

6
No escape
❀

When Zeena had gone, Ethan and Mattie stood in silence for a moment. Then Mattie began to tidy the kitchen and Ethan went outside to check the animals, as he did every night. The room was empty when he returned, but on the table under his pipe was a piece of paper. Three words were written on it: 'Ethan, don't worry'.

There was a small room at the back of the house where Ethan kept his books and papers. His mother had let him use it as a study-room when he first returned to the farm after his father's accident. He still sat there in summer, but the room had no fire and in winter it was too cold. This was where he went to look again at his message from Mattie. It was the first time she had ever written to him. He read her words and felt nearer to her, but at the same time he remembered that very soon he would never see her again. 'Soon there'll be no warm smile, no gentle voice, only this – cold paper and dead words,' he thought.

He lay down on a hard little bed that was there, covered himself with an old coat, and began to think about his life. He had lost so many chances and forgotten so many of his dreams, all to please Zeena. But she was now far more discontented than when he had married her. Must he live the rest of his days beside this bitter, complaining woman? No. He was too young and strong, too full of life to throw away all hope of happiness. Then he thought – why shouldn't he leave with Mattie the next day? He would hide his suitcase under the seat of the sleigh, leave Zeena a letter . . .

He jumped up, lit the lamp again, sat down at the table and began to write.

Zeena, I've done everything I could for you. But it hasn't worked. It's neither my fault nor yours. Maybe it'll be better for both of us if we live apart. I'm going to see what I can find in the West. You can sell the farm and saw-mill and keep the money—

At that word, he stopped writing and began to think. Without the farm he would have no money. He was sure that he could find work in the West, but would he get enough money to take care of Mattie too? And what about Zeena, alone on the farm? She couldn't keep it going on her own, and it would be hard to sell. The land was poor and not many people would want to buy it. But how could he let poor Mattie leave alone?

As he picked up his pen, his eye fell on a Bettsbridge newspaper. He saw the words 'Journeys to the West', and pulled the lamp nearer to see the prices of the tickets. Then the pen fell from his hand, and he pushed the unfinished letter away. He didn't even have the money to take Mattie to the West. He had already borrowed to mend the saw-mill, and couldn't borrow any more. The cold facts closed around him like prison doors. There was no way out – none. He was locked in that prison for life, and now his one light was disappearing.

He lay down again with a heavy heart and tears burning in his eyes. Through the window he saw the snow-covered slopes shining in the moonlight, the silver-edged darkness of the woods, and the shadowy purple of the hills against the sky. He felt that the beauty of the night was laughing at him, lying there so miserably.

He fell asleep. In the morning he woke cold and hungry. He went to the window, and saw a red sun coming up over the grey edges of the fields. 'This is Matt's last day,' he said to himself. He tried to think how the place would be without her.

He heard a step behind him, turned round and saw Mattie. She looked so small and thin, standing there in her poor dress in the cold, wintry light.

'I'll come and light the kitchen fire,' he said.

Mattie started her usual morning housework. The kitchen slowly became warmer, and the first sunlight entered the room. Ethan began to feel more hopeful. 'Maybe Zeena didn't mean what she said,' he thought. 'Maybe, now that daylight's here, she'll think again and let Mattie stay.'

He went up to Mattie and touched her arm gently. 'I don't want you to worry, Matt,' he said, looking down into her eyes with a smile. 'I guess things'll be all right.'

'No, I ain't going to worry,' she said softly.

He went out to the farm, and soon afterwards Jotham Powell joined him. As they were doing their morning's work with the cows, Jotham said:

'Mrs Frome told me the new girl's comin' today, and

Mattie's leavin'. I got to take her down to the station.'

Ethan felt the blood beating in his head. After a moment he found his voice, and said:

'Oh, it ain't so sure that Mattie's going—'

'Is that so?' said Jotham, not at all interested, and he went on with his work.

When they returned to the kitchen, the two women were already at breakfast. Zeena was eating well, and seemed very lively and busy. She looked at the hired man.

'Jotham, I want you here mid-afternoon to pick up Mattie,'

Zeena was eating well, and seemed very lively and busy.

she said. 'The new girl's getting to the station at five o'clock. Mattie can get the train at six.' Then she turned to Mattie and went on, 'Now, what've you done with one of my best cotton sheets? And there are a few other things missing, too.'

Mattie followed Zeena out of the room, leaving the two men alone.

'I guess I'll come round mid-afternoon, then,' said Jotham to his employer.

When the morning's work was finished, Ethan said to Jotham: 'I'm going down to Starkfield. Tell them not to wait for me at dinnertime.'

It was a clear, still morning, with a whisper of spring in the air. The snowy fields shone silver in the bright morning sunlight. Ethan walked down the road, angry and ashamed. So Mattie really was leaving, and he could only stand by, helpless. What must she think of him? As he walked, he could feel Mattie in the fields and sky around him, and could hear her laughing voice in the song of the birds. He knew that he had to do something. But what?

Then a thought came to him. Andrew Hale was a kind-hearted man. 'Maybe,' thought Ethan, 'he'll let me have some money now, if I tell him that Zeena's really sick and that we need a hired girl to help her. Mrs Hale will listen to me, I'm sure.'

He thought about this idea as he walked faster and faster down the road. With each long step he felt more sure of his plan's success. And with fifty dollars in his pocket, nothing could keep him from Mattie . . .

As he came into Starkfield, he saw the Hales' sleigh, and hurried forward to meet it. The sleigh stopped, and Mrs Hale's round, motherly face looked out. She smiled at Ethan, told him that her husband was at home, then added:

'I'm sorry that Zeena's feeling bad again. She's lucky to have you to take care of her. And so was your poor mother. You've had an awful hard life, Ethan Frome.'

When she had gone, Ethan felt less alone in his unhappiness. It had been a long time since anyone had spoken to him as kindly as Mrs Hale. The Hales were caring people who felt sorry for him, and now he felt sure that they would help him.

He started down the road to their house, then stopped after a few steps. He suddenly saw himself, and his life, in the clear light of day. He was a poor man, planning to leave his sickly wife all alone and without money. And how was he planning to do this heartless thing? By telling lies to two kind people who felt sorry for him.

He turned and walked slowly back to the farm.

7
The last ride
※

It was about midday when Ethan got home. Zeena was by the fire with a scarf on her head and a book about stomach pains in her hand. She did not move or look up.

'Where's Mattie?' Ethan asked.

Zeena continued to read her book. 'I guess she's packing her case,' she replied.

Ethan went straight upstairs. Mattie's door was closed. 'Matt,' he said in a low voice. There was no answer, so he gently pushed open the door.

Mattie was sitting on her case in her best dress, with her back to the door and her face in her hands. She was crying. Ethan put his hands on her shoulders.

'Matt – oh, don't – oh, Matt!'

'Ethan – I thought you weren't coming back!' she cried, lifting her wet face to his.

He took her in his arms, and kissed her soft hair. Then they heard Zeena calling, and moved away from each other.

He carried her suitcase downstairs, and with every 'tick' of the clock, the pain in his heart grew.

At dinner he could eat nothing. After the meal Zeena sat down by the fire and Mattie began to wash the dishes. Jotham got up from the table and asked Ethan:

'So what time'll I come round for Mattie?'

'You needn't come round; I'm going to drive her over myself,' he answered.

Zeena lifted her head. 'I want you here this afternoon, Ethan. You'll have to get the room ready for the new girl. Jotham can take Mattie.'

'I'm going to drive her over myself,' he repeated in a hard voice. He turned to Mattie: 'You be ready at three, Matt. I've got business in Corbury.'

'I thought you weren't coming back!' Mattie cried.

With those words he left the house. He could feel the hot blood beating in his head, as the anger burned inside him. He hurried through his work, then went to get the horse and sleigh. He remembered the day when he had got the sleigh ready in order to fetch his wife's cousin from the station. It was little more than a year ago, on a soft afternoon just like this, with a whisper of spring in the air. And all the days between then and now came back to him, one by one.

He jumped into the sleigh and drove up to the house. The kitchen was empty, and Mattie's case and coat lay ready by the door. After a moment he heard someone moving about in his study-room. He pushed open the door and saw Mattie standing by the table.

'What are you doing in there, Matt?'

'Just looking round,' she replied.

'Where's Zeena?'

'Gone upstairs. She said she had her pains again.'

'Didn't she say goodbye?'

'No. That was all she said.'

They went back into the kitchen. Ethan looked slowly around the room, thinking, 'In a few hours I shall return here alone. I'm looking at Mattie here for the last time.' He could not believe it; it all seemed so unreal.

'Come on,' he said, opening the door. He helped her into the sleigh, and with a 'Go along!' to the horse, they started off down the hill.

'We got lots of time for a good ride, Matt!' he said, taking her hand in his.

As they left the farm, he did not take the road towards Starkfield, but turned the horse to the right, up the Bettsbridge road. Mattie did not seem surprised.

'Are you going round by Shadow Pond?'

'You knew, didn't you?' he laughed.

The road took them down into a wood, where the trees shone reddish in the afternoon sun, leaving soft blue shadows on the untouched snow. There was a warm stillness in the wood. In the middle was a small icy pond, with sweet-smelling trees all around. It was a quiet, secret place, like the quiet sadness in Ethan's heart. They saw a fallen tree by the icy water, half covered in snow. It was where they had sat once last August, together with a group of young people from Starkfield church.

They sat down now in the same place, and remembered those few happy moments from that hot summer afternoon. Ethan looked at Mattie's hair, and wished he could touch it again. He wanted to tell her that it smelled of the woods in

It was where they had once sat last August . . .

45

springtime, but he had never learned to say things like that.

When the sun began to go down behind the hill, Mattie said: 'We mustn't stay here any longer.'

As they drove back towards Starkfield, the sky was turning grey, with a cold red over the western hills.

'Matt,' Ethan said at last. 'What'll you do? Can't you ask your father's family for help?'

'I don't want to ask them,' she replied, then after a moment added: 'I guess I'll find something.'

'You know I'd do anything for you—'

'Yes, I know.'

'But I can't—'

She was silent, but he felt her shoulder shaking. 'Oh, Matt,' he cried. 'I wish . . .'

She turned to him. 'Ethan, I found this.' She held out a piece of paper. It was the unfinished letter to his wife, which he had forgotten to destroy. A painful happiness ran through him. Were Mattie's dreams the same as his? He had to know.

'Do you feel like that too, Matt? Tell me, Matt, tell me!'

'Oh, Ethan, what does it matter now?' she cried. With a sudden movement she tore the letter into pieces and threw them onto the snow. For a moment she was silent, then said in a low voice:

'The first time I thought of you like that was at Shadow Pond. Then I often used to think about you on summer nights when the moon was too bright and I couldn't sleep.'

Her words filled Ethan's heart with sweetness. Darkness began to fall and they drove on in silence for a while.

Mattie tore the letter into pieces and threw them onto the snow.

'I'm fastened hand and foot, Matt. There isn't a thing I can do,' he began again.

'You must write to me sometimes, Ethan.'

'Oh, what can writing do? I want to put my hand out and touch you. I want to take care of you. I want to be there when you're sick and when you're lonely.'

'Oh, Ethan, I wish I was dead!' she cried.

'Don't let's talk that way,' he whispered.

As they arrived in Starkfield, a sleigh with bells passed them. They heard happy children's voices and saw a group of village boys with sleds. They drove on to the top of the Corbury road. On one side was the tall white shape of the church, on the other were the dark shadows of the Varnum trees. The steep slope lay empty and white below them. An

47

idea came to Ethan, to help himself and her through their miserable last hour. He turned to Mattie.

'We never went coasting last night. Shall we go down now? How would you like that?'

'There isn't time!'

'There's as much time as we want,' he said. 'The hired girl can wait. Look, someone's left a sled under the trees.'

He helped her out of the sleigh, and took her by the hand towards the sled. They both sat down on it, with Mattie in front and Ethan behind.

The steep slope lay empty and white below them.

'It's so dark, Ethan. Are you sure you can see?'

'Oh, I can do this with my eyes closed!' he laughed. She laughed with him, then after a moment he cried: 'Now!'

They started off, and soon the sled was flying down the slope, round the corner by the big tree, and down the second slope. They came to a stop, picked up the sled, and began to climb up the hill again.

'It was wonderful!' laughed Mattie.

'Weren't you afraid when we went round the tree?'

'I'm never afraid with you,' she replied.

A deep silence seemed to fall from the starless sky. At each step of their climb Ethan said to himself: 'It's the last time we'll ever walk together.'

When they reached the Varnum trees, Ethan put back the sled. 'I guess this must be Ned Hale's sled,' he said.

'Is this where Ned and Ruth kissed each other?' Mattie whispered, throwing her arms round Ethan. Her lips found his, and Ethan held her close to him.

'Goodbye – goodbye,' she said in a shaking voice, and kissed him again.

'Matt, I can't let you go! What'll we do? What'll we do?'

They stood holding hands like children. Through the stillness they heard the church clock.

'Oh, Ethan, it's already five o'clock. It's time!'

'Time for what? I'm not leaving you now. How can we go anywhere without each other, after this?'

Suddenly she threw her arms round his neck again.

'Ethan! Ethan! I want you to take me down again!'

'Down where?'

'Down there. Into the tree, to finish it all. Then we'll never have to leave each other again.'

'Matt! What are you saying? Are you crazy?'

'No, but I will be crazy if I leave you. Where'll I go without you? You're the only person who's ever been good to me. And there'll be a strange girl sleeping in my bed where I used to lie at night and think of you . . .'

Her words were like pieces torn from his heart. Now at last he knew that Mattie's feelings were as strong as his. How could he go back to that hated house, to the woman who was waiting for him there?

He held her close and kissed her, but when her face touched his, it was cold and wet with tears. He saw the road down to the station, and through the still air he heard a train. The dark trees covered them in blackness and silence, like a grave. 'Perhaps it'll be like this,' he thought. 'After this I won't feel anything.'

'Come,' she whispered, pulling at his hand. He picked the sled up, and they took their places on it. This time he made her sit behind him. She put her arms round him, and he turned his head and kissed her. She was right – this was better than being apart.

Just as they started, he heard his horse whinny. First came the steep drop, and they seemed to be flying through the air, high up into the cloudy night. Then Ethan saw the big tree at the corner of the road, and he said between his teeth: 'We can do it; I know we can do it—'

'We can do it; I know we can do it—'

As they flew towards the tree, Mattie held him closer and he seemed to feel her heart beating. The tree became bigger and nearer. 'It's waiting for us; it knows,' he thought. But suddenly his wife's face, grim and twisted, appeared before him, and he moved to push the picture away. There was a last moment when the air shot past him like millions of burning stars. And then the tree . . .

The sky was still cloudy, but when he looked straight up he saw a single star. What was its name? He used to know, but he couldn't remember. He felt so tired . . . Through the deep stillness he heard a little animal making a small, frightened sound. He knew the animal was in terrible pain – he could feel its pain shooting through his own body. He reached out his left arm to help the poor animal, and felt something soft under his hand. He tried to move but could not, because there was a rock, or some heavy thing, lying on him. Then he realized that his hand was on Mattie's face, and the sound was coming from her lips . . .

He put his face next to hers, and in the darkness he saw her eyes open and heard her say his name.

'Oh, Matt, I thought we'd done it,' he whispered; and far away, up the hill, he heard the horse whinny, and thought: 'I ought to give him his supper . . .'

8
Endings

The whining voice stopped as I stepped into Frome's kitchen. There were two women sitting there, and I could not tell which one had been the speaker.

One of them stood up when we entered, and without a

There were two women sitting there.

word went to bring a dish of food to the table. She was tall and thin, and wore an untidy, shapeless dress. Her lined face and thin lips were of the same yellowish colour, and she had thin grey hair and grey, lifeless eyes.

The other woman was smaller, and she also had grey hair and a thin, bloodless face. She turned her head towards me quickly, but her body did not move at all. Her dark eyes shone with the crazy brightness that is sometimes seen in people with disease of the spine.

The kitchen was a poor place. The few pieces of furniture were of the poorest kind, mostly broken and dirty.

'My, it's cold in here,' said Frome, looking around.

The tall woman said nothing, but the dark-eyed woman answered complainingly, in a thin, whining voice:

'It's Zeena's fault. She fell asleep and the fire went out. I've been so cold, waiting for her to wake up.'

I knew then that it was her voice that I had heard.

The tall woman brought the food to the table. Frome looked at me and said: 'This is my wife, Mrs Frome.' After a moment he added, turning to the figure in the armchair: 'And this is Miss Mattie Silver . . .'

Ruth Hale was very pleased to see me return safely in the morning, and most surprised to hear how I had spent the night.

'You must be the first stranger there in twenty years,' she said. 'It's awful to see them, all locked up together in that house. And they're not easy people, any of them. Mattie used to be; before the accident she was a really sweet girl. But not now – she's had too much pain. Now, when she and Zeena fight, the look on Ethan's face is enough to break your heart.'

'Yes, it must be awful for them,' I agreed.

'It was just terrible at the beginning,' she went on. 'They brought Mattie here, and I stayed with her all night. Then in the morning she opened her eyes and said . . . Oh, I don't know why I'm telling you this . . .' She stopped, crying.

After a few moments she dried her tears and continued: 'Then when the doctors said we could move Mattie, Zeena sent for her and took her back to the farm.'

'And she's been there ever since?' I asked.

'There was no other place for her to go,' Ruth Hale answered simply; and I thought how hard life was for the poor.

'Zeena's cared for the pair of them for over twenty years now,' Ruth Hale went on. 'And there they all are, shut up in that one kitchen.'

Then she looked at me and said in a low voice:

'There was one day, about a week after the accident, when they thought Mattie couldn't live. Well, I say it was a pity she did. People think that's an awful thing to say, but they weren't with her when she first woke up . . . And I say this, too. All those years with Mattie have destroyed Ethan.

The way they are now, there's not much difference between the Fromes up at the farm and the Fromes down in their graves – except that down there they're all silent and the women have to keep quiet.'

GLOSSARY

anger   the feeling when you are angry

apart   not together

beauty   being beautiful

bitter   angry and unhappy about something that has happened

buggy   a small, open 'car' with four wheels, pulled by a horse

coasting   riding down a snow-covered hill on a sled

complain   to say that you are not happy about something

cousin   the son or daughter of your aunt or uncle

despair   the feeling when you have lost all hope

difference   being different

discontented   not happy, not pleased

dish *(n)*   a plate or bowl for holding food, fruit, etc.

embarrassed   feeling shy or uncomfortable; worrying about
  what other people will think

fault   when something bad or wrong happens because of what
  you have done, it is your fault

flow   to move like water

further   the opposite of 'nearer'

glue *(n)*   something soft and sticky used to join things together

grave *(n)*   a hole in the ground where a dead person's body is put

gravestone   a stone on a grave, with the name, dates, etc. of the
  dead person

grim   very serious-looking, unsmiling

hire   to pay to use something, or to use someone's help

housekeeper   a person who takes care of someone's home

jealous   angry or sad because you are afraid of losing someone's
  love or because you want what another person has

jug   a pot with a handle, for things like milk, water, etc.

kiss *(v)* to touch someone with your lips in a loving way

lamp something that gives light

lined having long, thin marks on your face, like an old person

lively full of life

load *(v)* to put things (often large and heavy) into a car, ship, etc.

mail *(n)* (*American English*) post (letters, postcards, etc.)

maybe perhaps

pond a very small lake

poverty being very poor

rocking chair a chair on rockers, which can be moved backwards and forwards by the person sitting in it

saw mill a kind of small factory where trees and wood are cut

scarf a piece of cloth to wear round the head or neck

science the study of natural things in the world

sew to join pieces of cloth together; to make or mend clothes

silence *(n)* being silent

sled a kind of small, open 'car' without wheels, but with long pieces of metal or wood for moving over snow

sleigh a large sled, pulled by a horse

slope the side of a hill; a piece of ground that goes up or down

smart *(adj)* (*American English*) clever

spine the long, thin bone down the middle of your back

steep *(adj)* going up or down very quickly, e.g. a steep hill

tear (past tense **tore**) to pull something (e.g. paper) into pieces

thought *(n)* something that you think

twisted *(adj)* pulled into a strange shape

warmth a warm feeling

whine *(v)* to speak in a thin, high, complaining voice

whinny *(v)* to make the long high cry of a horse

NON-STANDARD ENGLISH USED IN THIS STORY

ain't   am not / isn't / aren't; hasn't / haven't
awful cold, awful hard   awfully (very) cold, awfully hard
I got   I have got
comin', leavin'   coming, leaving

ACTIVITIES

Before Reading

1 Read the story introduction on the first page of the book, and the back cover. What kind of story do you think *Ethan Frome* will be? Use this table to make some sentences.

		funny story.
		serious story.
		frightening story.
		fall in love with Mattie.
	it will be a	marry Mattie.
I think		become very rich.
	Ethan will	stay with his wife.
I don't think		leave his wife.
	it will end	try to kill his wife.
		try to kill himself.
		happily.
		sadly.

2 Why do you think life was so hard for a poor farmer in Massachusetts a hundred years ago? Do country people have easier lives today? Make some sentences using these ideas.

- horses / modern machinery
- help from the government / help from your family
- long cold winters / illness / travelling difficult

While Reading

Read Chapter 1. Match these people with the sentences.

Ruth Hale / Denis Eady / Harmon Gow / Ethan Frome /
the narrator (the person telling the story)

1 _____ told the narrator about Ethan Frome's accident.
2 _____ was staying in Starkfield because of his work.
3 _____ lived in the finest house in the village.
4 _____ was a successful Starkfield businessman.
5 _____ drove the narrator to the station in his sleigh.

At the end of Chapter 1, the narrator knew the answer to only one of these questions. Which one? Can you guess the answers to the other two?

1 Why was Ethan's body so damaged?
2 Why did Ethan's face have a sad, grim look all the time?
3 Whose was the whining voice in Ethan's house?

Read Chapters 2 and 3, and then answer these questions.

1 Who danced with a pretty girl in Starkfield church?
2 Who brought hope, life and brightness into Ethan's home?
3 Who went to Bettsbridge to see a new doctor?
4 Who drove his employer's wife to the station?
5 Who said he could not pay Ethan at the moment?
6 Who kissed her boyfriend under the trees by her home?

Match these halves of sentences about Chapter 3, and join them with these linking words.

and so / and then / because / but / in order to / when

1 Ethan left his engineering studies and came home . . .
2 His father died, . . .
3 His cousin Zeena came to the farm . . .
4 After his mother died, Ethan was afraid of being alone . . .
5 They wanted to sell the farm and move to the town, . . .
6 Mattie Silver came to live with them . . .
7 _____ his mother grew more and more silent and crazy.
8 _____ his father had had a bad accident.
9 _____ then Zeena became sickly and silent too.
10 _____ he asked Zeena to marry him.
11 _____ help Zeena with the housework.
12 _____ old Mrs Frome was dying.

Read Chapters 4 to 6. Choose the best question-word for these questions, and then answer them.

What / Why

1 . . . was Ethan looking forward to an evening at home?
2 . . . fell off the table and broke on the floor?
3 . . . was Mattie so worried about it?
4 . . . did Ethan and Mattie talk about that evening?
5 . . . did Ethan kiss?
6 . . . did Ethan take so long to come home with the glue?
7 . . . was the news about Zeena's health?
8 . . . was Ethan so angry about the hired girl?

9 ... did Zeena say Mattie had to leave?

10 ... wouldn't Mattie be able to find work in the town?

11 ... was Ethan planning to do before he saw the cost of tickets to the West?

12 ... do you think Zeena seemed so lively and busy?

13 ... didn't Ethan ask the Hales to lend him money?

Before you read Chapter 7 (*The Last Ride*), can you guess the answers to these questions?

1 Will Ethan think of another way to get some money?

2 Will Mattie leave Starkfield alone, or with Ethan?

3 Whose ride do you think it will be? Where to? Why?

Read Chapter 7. What does the word 'it' mean in these sentences?

1 It was a quiet, secret place, like the quiet sadness in Ethan's heart.

2 'It was wonderful!' laughed Mattie.

3 'Perhaps it'll be like this,' he thought. 'After this I won't feel anything.'

4 'Oh, Matt, I thought we'd done it,' he whispered.

Read Chapter 8, and then answer these questions.

1 Whose was the whining voice in Ethan's house?

2 Why had Mattie had to stay with the Fromes?

3 Ruth Hale spoke of the Fromes 'up at the farm' and 'down in their graves'. Which did she think were luckier?

After Reading

1 **Choose the best words to complete this text about Zeena.**

tall / lively / young / silent / shining / cold / thin / soft /
milky white / grey / dark / yellowish / whining / sweet /
smiles / complains / her own ill health / the beauty of nature

Zeena is a _____, _____ woman, with _____ eyes and ____
lips. Her hair is _____, and her skin is _____. Zeena has a
_____ voice, and she _____ a lot. She loves talking
about_____.

Now use the rest of the words to write a text about Mattie.

2 **Imagine that Mattie wrote to a friend about her problem.**
Complete her letter (use as many words as you like).

Dear Jessie,
Please help me, I just don't know _____! I'm so in love with
Ethan, and I think he feels _____. Last night he _____ from
a dance, and when we stood together in the moonlight,
he _____, I'm sure. But _____ has noticed something, and
I'm so afraid that she'll _____. Oh, what can I do? Should I
tell Ethan _____? Or should I keep quiet? Or marry Denis,
the shopkeeper's boring son? Maybe I should _____? But
where could I go? Oh, Jessie, please _____ soon!
Your dear friend, Mattie

3 How would *you* reply to Mattie's letter? Write and tell her what you think she should do. Use these phrases.

   • I think you should / ought to . . .
   • I don't think you should / ought to . . .
   • Why don't you . . . ?

4 When the narrator asked Ruth Hale about Ethan's accident, perhaps their conversation continued like this. Put the conversation in the right order, and write in the speakers' names. Ruth Hale speaks first (number 5.)

   1 _____ 'No, she was a Bettsbridge girl. Her father used to own a big company in town, but Mattie didn't have a dollar in her pocket when Zeena brought her here.'

   2 _____ 'So Mattie was in the accident as well?'

   3 _____ 'It was Mattie Silver, his wife's cousin.'

   4 _____ 'So she had to go and live with the Fromes?'

   5 _____ 'Yes, I knew them both . . . it was awful . . .'

   6 _____ 'Was she from Starkfield too?'

   7 _____ 'Silver was a bad businessman. He borrowed a lot, but couldn't pay it back. When he died, Mattie was left with nothing at all, and nobody to help her.'

   8 _____ 'Both? Who was the other person?'

   9 _____ 'Oh yes, she was hurt worse than Ethan. She can't walk at all, poor girl. Never leaves the house.'

   10 _____ 'What happened to her father's money?'

   11 _____ 'That's right. Twenty-five years she's been there now – twenty-four since the accident.'

5 **A police inspector questioned Jotham Powell about what happened at the Frome farm in the days before the accident. Complete the inspector's side of the conversation.**

INSPECTOR: So, Mr Powell, _____?

JOTHAM: Wednesday? Yes, I remember. Mr Frome and I were down at the saw-mill early, loading wood for Mr Hale.

INSPECTOR: And _____?

JOTHAM: About midday, I guess. Then Mr Frome and I went up to the house for a bite to eat.

INSPECTOR: _____?

JOTHAM: Yes, sir, they were both there. Miss Mattie was making coffee, and Mrs Frome was dressed in her travelling clothes, ready to leave for the station.

INSPECTOR: _____?

JOTHAM: Yes, I did. She caught the two o'clock train.

INSPECTOR: _____?

JOTHAM: No, I didn't see him again. I called in for a drop of coffee later, but Miss Mattie was alone then.

INSPECTOR: _____?

JOTHAM: She came home on Thursday. Mr Frome sent me to the station to fetch her after dinner.

INSPECTOR: _____?

JOTHAM: Well, on Friday morning Mrs Frome said I had to take Mattie to the station, and bring back the new girl.

INSPECTOR: _____?

JOTHAM: Because at dinner Mr Frome said he'd drive Miss Mattie to the station himself.

6 Here is a report of the accident in the newspaper. Correct the mistakes in the report, and think of a suitable title for it.

Two young people were killed on a coasting slope last Friday evening. The accident happened at about ten o'clock on a hillside in Corbury. Mr Ethan Frome, a Starkfield builder, and his cousin, Miss Mattie Silver, were on their way back from a dance. Mr Frome, who had never coasted before, went down a steep slope, with Miss Silver sitting in front of him on the sled. Half way down, the sled crashed into a big rock. Several people saw the accident.

7 Look at these ideas about the story.

1 It was Zeena's fault. She was cold, bitter, and jealous, and only cared about herself.
2 It was Mattie's fault. She was young and pretty, and she tried to take Ethan away from his wife, which was a very bad thing to do.
3 It was Ethan's fault. He was older than Mattie, and knew more about life than she did. He knew it was a stupid thing to do.
4 It was nobody's fault. It all happened because of their poverty. Poverty brought them all together to begin with, and poverty was their prison to the end.

Decide which of the ideas above is closest to . . .
 a) what Ruth Hale thought.
 b) what the narrator thought.
 c) what *you* think.

ABOUT THE AUTHOR

Edith Wharton was born Edith Newbold Jones in 1862 in New York. Her family was wealthy, and very much part of New York's fashionable society. Edith did not go to school, but was taught privately at home, where she also spent many hours reading in her father's library. In 1885 she married Edward Wharton, but their marriage was not a happy one. They divorced in 1913.

By 1907 Edith Wharton was living in France, first in Paris, which she loved, and later, in homes near Paris and on the Mediterranean coast. She had a wide circle of writer and artist friends, and Henry James, a famous novelist, was a close friend for many years. She died in the south of France in 1937.

Her first book, *The Decoration of Houses* (1897), written with an architect friend, was non-fiction, but this was followed by short stories and novels, including her first popular success, *The House of Mirth*, in 1905. She went on to write more than forty books, and in 1920 became the first woman to win the Pulitzer Prize, for her novel *The Age of Innocence*.

She wrote *Ethan Frome* (1911) while living in France, but she had learnt about New England farming life when she lived in Massachusetts for a few years after her marriage. Nearly all her other novels are about the comfortable world of the rich, but *Ethan Frome* describes the hard, hopeless lives of the very poor. The novel was very successful when first published, and has been popular ever since. A film of the story, starring Liam Neeson, was made in 1993.

OXFORD BOOKWORMS LIBRARY

Classics • Crime & Mystery • Factfiles • Fantasy & Horror
Human Interest • Playscripts • Thriller & Adventure
True Stories • World Stories

The OXFORD BOOKWORMS LIBRARY provides enjoyable reading in English, with a wide range of classic and modern fiction, non-fiction, and plays. It includes original and adapted texts in seven carefully graded language stages, which take learners from beginner to advanced level. An overview is given on the next pages.

All Stage 1 titles are available as audio recordings, as well as over eighty other titles from Starter to Stage 6. All Starters and many titles at Stages 1 to 4 are specially recommended for younger learners. Every Bookworm is illustrated, and Starters and Factfiles have full-colour illustrations.

The OXFORD BOOKWORMS LIBRARY also offers extensive support. Each book contains an introduction to the story, notes about the author, a glossary, and activities. Additional resources include tests and worksheets, and answers for these and for the activities in the books. There is advice on running a class library, using audio recordings, and the many ways of using Oxford Bookworms in reading programmes. Resource materials are available on the website <www.oup.com/bookworms>.

The *Oxford Bookworms Collection* is a series for advanced learners. It consists of volumes of short stories by well-known authors, both classic and modern. Texts are not abridged or adapted in any way, but carefully selected to be accessible to the advanced student.

You can find details and a full list of titles in the *Oxford Bookworms Library Catalogue* and *Oxford English Language Teaching Catalogues*, and on the website <www.oup.com/bookworms>.

THE OXFORD BOOKWORMS LIBRARY
GRADING AND SAMPLE EXTRACTS

STARTER • 250 HEADWORDS

present simple – present continuous – imperative – *can/cannot*, *must* –
going to (future) – simple gerunds ...

Her phone is ringing – but where is it?

Sally gets out of bed and looks in her bag. No phone.
She looks under the bed. No phone. Then she looks behind
the door. There is her phone. Sally picks up her phone and
answers it. *Sally's Phone*

STAGE 1 • 400 HEADWORDS

... past simple – coordination with *and, but, or* –
subordination with *before, after, when, because, so* ...

I knew him in Persia. He was a famous builder and I
worked with him there. For a time I was his friend, but
not for long. When he came to Paris, I came after him
– I wanted to watch him. He was a very clever, very
dangerous man. *The Phantom of the Opera*

STAGE 2 • 700 HEADWORDS

... present perfect – *will* (future) – *(don't) have to, must not, could* –
comparison of adjectives – simple *if* clauses – past continuous –
tag questions – *ask/tell* + infinitive ...

While I was writing these words in my diary, I decided what
to do. I must try to escape. I shall try to get down the wall
outside. The window is high above the ground, but I have
to try. I shall take some of the gold with me – if I escape,
perhaps it will be helpful later. *Dracula*

STAGE 3 • 1000 HEADWORDS

... should, may – present perfect continuous – *used to* – past perfect –
causative – relative clauses – indirect statements ...

Of course, it was most important that no one should see
Colin, Mary, or Dickon entering the secret garden. So Colin
gave orders to the gardeners that they must all keep away
from that part of the garden in future. *The Secret Garden*

STAGE 4 • 1400 HEADWORDS

*... past perfect continuous – passive (simple forms) –
would* conditional clauses – indirect questions –
relatives with *where/when* – gerunds after prepositions/phrases ...

I was glad. Now Hyde could not show his face to the world
again. If he did, every honest man in London would be
proud to report him to the police. *Dr Jekyll and Mr Hyde*

STAGE 5 • 1800 HEADWORDS

... future continuous – future perfect –
passive (modals, continuous forms) –
would have conditional clauses – modals + perfect infinitive ...

If he had spoken Estella's name, I would have hit him. I was
so angry with him, and so depressed about my future, that I
could not eat the breakfast. Instead I went straight to the old
house. *Great Expectations*

STAGE 6 • 2500 HEADWORDS

... passive (infinitives, gerunds) – advanced modal meanings –
clauses of concession, condition

When I stepped up to the piano, I was confident. It was as if I
knew that the prodigy side of me really did exist. And when
I started to play, I was so caught up in how lovely I looked
that I didn't worry how I would sound. *The Joy Luck Club*

BOOKWORMS • CLASSICS • STAGE 3

The Call of the Wild

JACK LONDON

Retold by Nick Bullard

When men find gold in the frozen north of Canada, they need dogs – big, strong dogs to pull the sledges on the long journeys to and from the gold mines.

Buck is stolen from his home in the south and sold as a sledge-dog. He has to learn a new way of life – how to work in harness, how to stay alive in the ice and the snow . . . and how to fight. Because when a dog falls down in a fight, he never gets up again.

BOOKWORMS • HUMAN INTEREST • STAGE 3

Love Story

ERICH SEGAL

Retold by Rosemary Border

This is a love story you won't forget. Oliver Barrett meets Jenny Cavilleri. He plays sports, she plays music. He's rich, and she's poor. They argue, and they fight, and they fall in love.

So they get married, and make a home together. They work hard, they enjoy life, they make plans for the future. Then they learn that they don't have much time left.

Their story has made people laugh, and cry, all over the world.